GREEK MYTHOLOGY

A Concise Guide to Ancient Gods, Heroes,
Beliefs and Myths

Table of Contents

Introduction

"Man: a being in search of meaning."

—Plato; a philosopher c428-348BCE

If you look back on the events of your day today, I am prepared to guess that you referenced Greek mythology at least twice, if not three times. Perhaps you are laughing, but think back: did you look at your horoscope under your sign of the *Zodiac?* Did you work like a *Spartan* to catch up on some work? Was your PC at work attacked by a *Trojan* virus? Did you order something via *Amazon.com?* Did you buy some household shopping at lunch time and pick up a bottle of *Ajax?* Perhaps you found a second-hand copy of *"The Tanglewood Tales"* by Nigel Hawthorne for your niece's birthday while you were out booking tickets to go to *"Orpheus in the Underworld"* on Saturday. Afterwards you might have wondered what it would be like to be *"as rich as Croesus"!* Television news channels today are discussing whether China and the United States are going to fall into the *Thucydides' Trap* - Thucydides being a famous Greek military leader who wrote about "the likelihood of conflict between a rising power and a currently dominant one."

All the many ancient civilizations that have come before us have left traces of the mythologies that guided them - but none more so than the Greeks. In common with other mythologies, early Greek mythology was handed down through the oral tradition of travelling bards from Minoa, Mycenae and Mesopotamia, re-telling tales that go back as far as 2700 BCE, like the epic of Gilgamesh, the semi-mythic King of Uruk. The Greeks also have one of the most complicated mythological systems, rife with some anomalies as well. While it's not perhaps the oldest, running from approximately 2000 BCE till the end of the Hellenistic era around c146 BCE, it is well-documented nevertheless. We know a great deal about it mostly through ancient pottery of all things; the ancient Egyptians may have inscribed their beliefs on the interior walls of their incredible burial sites. But the customs of the Greeks survived best on bits of decorated pottery in the form of vases, urns and pots that have defied the ravages of eons. Pottery survived, sometimes even intact, better than built structures and paintings, and these objects were decorated with abstract designs as well as realistic depictions of everyday life. The best-known style was the silhouetted, black figures in action, for example a vase by the potter Exekias depicting Achilles killing the Amazon Penthesilia dated 540 BCE.

What was different about Greek mythology though was the emphasis on the written record. This was a result of an unusual leaning towards the dramatic arts of rhetoric, poetics and theatrical performances as well as gifted historians like Herodotus (484–425 BCE) and Thucydides (460-395 BCE). Our ancestors have always endeavoured to keep records of events, for example the so-called *Doomsday Book*, but the Greeks were the first important civilization to translate these lists of happenings into written history with a narrative attached – often dramatized – which allows us to witness our past today. The fact that so much Greek custom and culture was subsumed in the wave of Roman influence as the Roman Empire advanced across the ancient world has had the odd effect of highlighting many aspects of Grecian life instead of obliterating it. One just has to remember the Roman aristocrat Publius Ovidius Naso (43 BCE–17 CE) to appreciate this. He is better remembered as Ovid, the poet who based his work on Greek and Roman mythology. His *Metamorphosis* would become one of Shakespeare's most fruitful story sources. This brief guide will cover the rise of Greece and biographies of selected gods from its colourful pantheon. I will touch on the ways Greek mythology is different from other popular mythologies and recount some key aspects of their beliefs. The adventures, triumphs and sorrows of their heroes and heroines are told in dramatic plays that still grip modern audiences today. This is as a result of one of the most interesting gods of all times; Dionysus, twice-born son of the great Zeus.

Ulysses

Myth is the nothing that is all
The very sun that breaks through the skies
Is a bright and speechless myth-
God's dead body,
Naked and alive.

This hero who cast anchor here,
Because he never was, slowly came to exist.
Without ever being, he sufficed us.
Having never come here,
He came to be our founder.

Thus the legend, little by little,
Seeps into reality
And constantly enriches it.
Life down below, half
Of nothing, perishes.

—Fernando Pessoa 1888-1935

Chapter One

What Is A Myth?

And why do we have them anyway? There are many definitions according to scholars: *"Myth is a traditional tale with secondary, partial reference to something of collective importance,"* according to Walter Burkert. *"A myth is a socially traditional story,"* according to Stephen Kershaw. Notice that neither scholar mentions "truth." Even so, it is a mistake to equate a myth with a "lie" or an untruth. Remember that we look back on ancient times and think about myths as stories or beliefs, but in the time of our ancestors the "myth" was their reality. So why were they constructed? The general consensus is that we created myths to explain our environment to ourselves and to make sense of our experiences, to answer the question about where we came from, who we are and how we can be happy. One can think of mythology as the forerunner of what we came to call philosophy, which is why myths are so entangled with religion and existentialism - and why they are so important. Myths are also how we recall historical events. It is incredible to think of all the history of the ancient world held in so fragile a vessel as the human mind!

Greece is located in southern Europe and is a peninsula and a surrounding archipelago enclosed on three sides by the Ionian, Aegean and Mediterranean Seas. Indo-European people, Minoan and Mycenaean, migrated into the area from c2000 BCE, settling successfully on the mainland and scattered islands. The legendary King Minos built a magnificent palace at Knossos on Crete, which grew to become the center of the Minoan Empire. The settlers were mainly pastoral farmers and crop growers who were organized into immensely independent and resourceful groups of families. The progress of these family groups was disrupted by a Dorian invasion, bringing a dark age to the region for nearly 500 years until the emergence of what would be a celebrated time of highly civilized city-states known as the Classical period, which ended in c336 BCE. The exploits of Alexander the Great as he set about conquering the world disrupted Greece and Thebes fell to him in c335 BCE, marking the start of the Hellenistic period lasting until c146 BCE.

It is virtually impossible to estimate the Greek population during this historic period. The best guess for the 5th century BCE is anywhere between 800,000 to 3 million people. What is certain though is that ancient Greece is regarded as the cradle of mankind in terms of art, culture and democracy - and that is why there is still an intense interest in the mythology of these times.

"Bury my body and don't build any monument.

Keep my hands out so the people know the one who won
the world
had nothing in hand when he died."

—Alexander the Great 356–323BCE

Chapter Two

The Sources Of Greek Mythology

The Greeks were polytheistic and as a result of the extensive and varied geographical nature of the burgeoning civilization, the myths that evolved included many variations–even more than usually expected in an oral tradition. There was no *one* sacred text to follow and no formal religious or social structure – each little settlement or village had their own favorite gods, and sometimes there were conflicting interpretations of popular myths. Mythography was certainly taught at schools, and by 500 BCE there were "handbooks" of myths collected by various people. There are several ancient texts which are pivotal to our understanding of this time. One of the most important, *"The Iliad,"* is an epic poem written in 750 BCE by Homer. It recounts the story of the end of the Trojan War and is one of the major sources for our understanding of the times. Homer's other great work. *"The Odyssey."* Takes place after the fall of Troy and tells the story of Odysseus' fantastic voyage home to his wife Penelope. Incredibly these magnificent sources have come down to us in their entirety. Hesiod, a contemporary of Homer and a fellow poet, he presents an incredibly detailed genealogy of the gods from Khaos to Polydoros in "Theogony," which features a vivid description of the creation of the universe as well as the events of the war with the Titans. A second work by Hesiod, *"Works and Days,"* covers human life and moral values through stories of well-known mythical figures like Prometheus and Pandora, offers advice on farming, and explains lucky days and unlucky days.

Lyric poetry was also abundant during this time. A poem like *"He is more than a hero"* by Sappho (c610–c570 BCE) captures the personal nature of the "myths" and the ambivalent sexuality that formed part of Grecian life.

He is more than a hero
he is a god in my eyes—
the man who is allowed
to sit beside you –

he who listens intimately
to the sweet murmur of
your voice, the enticing

laughter that makes my own
heart beat fast. If I meet
you suddenly, I can't

speak — my tongue is broken;
a thin flame runs under
my skin; seeing nothing,

hearing only my own ears
drumming, I drip with sweat;
trembling shakes my body

and I turn paler than
dry grass. At such times
death isn't far from me.

Pindar (c522–c438 BCE) was probably the greatest lyrical poet and specialized in large-scale choral odes often celebrating Olympian athletic victories. He was also known to have "corrected" written copies of traditional mythology.

Apollonius of Rhodes was probably born somewhere in the first half of the third century BCE and supplies an excellent source on the myth of Jason and the Golden Fleece in his work *Argonautica*. He is sometimes mistaken for the erudite Grecian scholar, Apollodorus, who was born in c130 BCE and is best known for his "*Chronicle of Greek History*."

The philosophers of the Classical Period also supply some information on the mythography of Greece albeit, more negative information than positive. Socrates (c469–399 BCE) is said to be the father of philosophy, a controversial figure in Greek history, he was a gifted teacher. His pedagogical style was to ask questions of his pupils and use their answers to improve their way of reasoning – a style still used today that bears his name, as it's commonly referred to as the Socratic Method. He was critical of the gods and went as far as to suggest that there might actually only *be* one god. When he heard that the Oracle at Delphi had apparently said he was the wisest man alive, Socrates was quite upset. One of the quotes attributed to him was: "*I can't teach anybody anything; I can only make them think.*" Socrates' greatest pupil, Plato (429-347 BCE) was openly scathing of Homer and Hesiod: "*These, methinks, composed false stories which they told and still tell to mankind.*" Aristotle (384-322 BCE) too was fairly dismissive of the school of Hesiod, saying *"about those who have invented clever mythologies it is not worthwhile to take a serious book."* It is therefore somewhat confusing to find that he wrote an entire book on the subject called *"Metaphysics,"* in which he expressed appreciation for the fact that great myths would often form the basis of philosophical formulations about the nature of being. *"It is the mark of an educated mind to be able to entertain a thought without accepting it,"* said Aristotle.

However, the most important source of information about the nature and place of Greek myths is however the work of the great dramatists of the Classical Age: Aeschylus, Sophocles, Euripides and Aristophanes. They deserve a much more in-depth look – more on them later.

"It lies in the lap of the gods."

—Homer

Chapter Three

The Creation Of The Universe And The Gods

The beginning of time is very murky in Greek mythology, with many variations of what is supposed to have happened, especially in the order of events. Rather than get bogged down in detail I have chosen to steer a middle path informed by hours of reading on the subject. In the beginning there was Khaos, was either a god itself *or* a set of circumstances. Our word "chaos" comes from this word. But in the tale of early Greek mythology it has a very different meaning: *a state of utter confusion or disorder; a total lack of organization or order.* In Greek mythology it was a "formless or void" state and has nothing to do with a great deal of noise and confusion. It was actually a gap or a space that existed, perhaps as a result of the separation of heaven and earth. From the depth of Khaos came Gaia i.e. the earth itself. Gaia was beautiful; she separated heaven from earth, water from land and air from space. She gave birth to Uranus (the sky) who in turn created rain to fashion the mountains, the rivers, the animals and the plants. Gaia also gave rise to Nyx (night), Pontus (the sea), Tartarus (the Underworld) and Erebus, the darkness that covers the Underworld. In some versions Gaia also gives birth to the goddess Aphrodite, who brings love and beauty into the world.

Gaia and Uranus mate to create their first of many children, the 12 Titans – huge and powerful gods, like Oceanus, who has thousands of children i.e. all the rivers of the world. Another Titian, Hyperion, is credited with the creation of Dawn, the Sun and the Moon. Significant of their offspring was Cronus, who will soon play a pivotal and painful part in this epic story. The second set of gods born from Gaia and Uranus are the Cyclopes; they are also huge and powerful and were the first blacksmiths. The three Cyclopes were known as Steropes, Brontes and Argus. Each had one fearful eye in the middle of his forehead and they were responsible for lightning, lightning bolts and thunder. The world was steadily becoming noisier. Uranus and Gaia had three more formidable children known as the Hecatoncheirs – each had a hundred hands and fifty heads and they were gigantic enough to hurl mountains around. Appropriately, they were in charge of earthquakes.

Uranus was actually a reasonable leader, and all the gods were fairly happy under his rule. However, Uranus himself developed an intense dislike of his own offspring which is not really explained in any way. He decided to stop his children from being and he shoved them unceremoniously back into Gaia's womb, interpreted as "hidden in secret parts of the earth." This infuriated her, and when her pleadings with him to relieve her of this pain and burden had no effect, she plotted with Cronus, one of her offspring, to punish Uranus for this cruelty.

The plan was devilish. When next Uranus came to lie with her, Cronus, presumably from inside his mother, cut off his father's genitals with a scythe and cast them, bleeding, onto the earth. *"And not vainly did they fall from his hand; for all the bloody drops that gushed forth Gaia received, and as the seasons moved round she bore the strong Erinyes and the great Gigantes...with gleaming armour, holding long spears in their hands and the Nymphai whom they call Meliai all over the boundless earth."* (Theogony by Hesiod) The Erinyes were the Fates or Furies, including gods like Poinai, Aroi and Praxidikai, whose three respective purviews were Retaliations, Curses and Exacting Justice. The Gigantes were a tribe of very strong giants and the cause of thermal activity and volcanoes. They included gods like Enkelades and Porphyrian. The Meliai were the honey-nurse nymphs of the god Zeus and perhaps even the nurses of mankind. In some versions the genitals are cast into the sea and Aphrodite, the goddess of love, is born from the foam that arises from the semen.

This would not be the only time a son usurps his father. A triumphant Cronus becomes king of the gods, frees all his siblings and marries Rhea. his sister. They produce six children; the gods Hestia, Demeter, Hera, Hades, Poseidon and Zeus. Somehow Cronus becomes aware of a prophecy that he will be unseated by one of his children, so each time one is born he swallows them alive. Rhea is desperate to save at least one of her children, and when Zeus is born she secretly sends him away to Crete to be brought up by nymphs. In his place, she wraps a large stone in swaddling clothes and hands it to Cronus, who promptly swallows it down.

Zeus grows up into a formidable warrior and lover and returns to Olympus as a cup bearer to Cronus. This allows him to slip Cronus the proverbial "Mickey Finn," a magic potion which causes him to regurgitate Zeus' siblings (as well as the rock representing Zeus). This rock, known as an omphalos stone, is enshrined at the Delphi Shrine to this day; while there are several explanations for this stone coming to reside at Delphi, this is but one of them.

In gratitude his siblings joined forces with Zeus against their father. This set up a simmering rivalry between the Olympian gods led by Zeus and the Titans led by Cronus. The resulting conflict is known as the Titanomachy, which lasted ten years. Eventually Zeus prevailed and the defeated Titans were banished to Tartarus with but a few exceptions. The Titan Atlas was tasked with holding the earth up safely on his shoulders; the Titan brothers Epimetheus and Prometheus, who had sided with Zeus, were tasked with creating the first mortal men instead of being banished.

The victorious Olympians retired to Mount Olympus and looked forward to a period of increased civilization. At about this time the very first Olympic Games were held. Only men were allowed to take part. Zeus married his sister Hera and he produced many more deities with her and in many other unions, the Graces, the Seasons and the Muses to mention a few. The relative peace did not last long, as the Giants taunted the Olympians by interfering in the running of the earth by diverting rivers, dislodging mountains and generally causing havoc until a great battle ensued: the Gigantomachy. Zeus reasserted his power as the king of the gods and restored the order of the universe. Zeus would be challenged yet again by the most feared god of all, the horrendous monster, Typhon, as tall as the stars and able to clasp the entire world in his hands. He had 100 dragons erupting from his neck with eyes that flashed fire and he was covered in wings. He was the product of the final mating of Gaia and Tartarus, and was determined to take over Mount Olympus. Zeus finally cornered him by using 100 lightning bolts at once and he placed Mount Etna over him to keep him in check. To this day mankind is threatened by Typhon, as the great beast tries to break free from his prison.

*"How the gods must have chuckled when they added
Hope to the evils
with which they filled Pandora's box, for they knew
very well
that this was the cruelest evil of them all, since it is
Hope that lures mankind to endure its misery to the
end."*

—W. Somerset Maugham; British author 1874–1965

Chapter Four

What Of Man? What Of Woman?

It may have struck you that all the gods had taken human form. This is one of the anomalies in Greek mythology; mortal man seems to have been very much an afterthought. They may have been created because the gods became tired of looking after themselves in terms of sustenance - they were perhaps created simply for the purposes of growing the crops that provided food, wine and fuel for fire for the gods. Some scholars suggest they were created simply as a diversion and amusement for the gods. They may have just provided extra fighting bodies for the gods in their endless battles. When Zeus appointed Prometheus and his brother Epimetheus to create men, his only stipulation had been that they should not have immortality.

It is interesting that Prometheus means "someone who evaluates before he acts" and Epimetheus means "someone who acts spontaneously and then evaluates." Prometheus tasked Epimetheus with creating many more creatures to inhabit the earth and equipping them with the various qualities and skills they needed to thrive and protect themselves: swiftness, strength, wings, claws, shells, cunning, fur etc. Prometheus in the meantime painstakingly fashioned man in clay and in the likeness of the gods. When he was finished, Epimetheus had used up all the special qualities and had nothing particular with which to endow man. Prometheus had acquired a fondness for the creature he was creating and decided the best he could do was to allow men to walk upright so that they could raise their eyes to heaven to praise the gods. He gave man the gift of fire as well. He then asked Athena to breathe life into man; this is how men came into existence. Zeus however was very displeased that man had acquired the gift of fire. In a fury he condemned Prometheus to be chained to a mountain for eternity. Every day a ferocious eagle would come to tear out and eat his liver. Because Prometheus he was immortal, his liver would regrow every night, dooming him go through the ordeal over and over. He was eventually rescued by the demigod Heracles.

Not content with Prometheus' punishment, and wanting to punish man as well, Zeus commanded Hephaestus to craft a woman so beautiful that she would "plague the hearts of men" forever. Although Hephaestus was the blacksmith of the gods, he was also a skilled craftsman and often produced decorative work of great beauty for the goddesses. The enchanting mortal, a female creature he fashioned from clay like man, was named Pandora, which means "the one who bears all gifts." Zeus commanded all the gods to each give her a gift which sounds very gracious until you hear that he instructed Hermes to teach her to be "deceitful, stubborn and curious."

Eventually the container, which might have been a box or more likely a storage jar, was filled with all the evils and miseries they could think of, including the plague and other contagious diseases, famine, poverty etc. It is clear that Zeus intended her as a punishment to mankind. She was instructed never to open the box under any circumstances and sent as a gift to wed Epimetheus. Initially Pandora obeyed the god's injunction, but eventually her curiosity got the better of her and she opened the box. She was overwhelmed by the horrible creatures that immediately escaped and spread around the entire world, bringing great harm. In a panic she slammed the lid down and, in one of the unfathomable ironies of the universe, the last creature, "Hope," was trapped inside the box.

Both Ovid and Hesiod talk about the ages of man. Ovid lists four ages and Hesiod, five. Neither list slips seamlessly into the generalized chronology of the creation of the universe. One must remember that all the sources of this ancient history were committed to writing hundreds of years after it was supposed to have taken place and by different writers, with different agendas at different times, so it is all a bit like the exegesis of the Christian scriptures. According to Hesiod the first age of man is known as their Golden Age and was a time when everyone lived in harmony and happiness. The animals could converse using human language. It was a time of abundance and even if death came, it came gently and at night when one was asleep. This was during the reign of Cronus. Then Cronus ate his children, which eventually caused the Titanomachy, and ten years of war brought this age to an end.

The gods then created the Silver Age of man. These mortals took a long time to grow up and never really matured. They remained very childish and disobedient, and would never pay proper heed to honoring the gods. Zeus became very impatient with their foolishness and destroyed them, sending their spirits to live in Hades.

Zeus soon grew bored without having mankind to toy with, so he created a brazen race of strong and warlike mortals. They were obsessed with weapons which they made of bronze; they built their homes of bronze as well - hence the Bronze Age of man. However they became consumed with their own aggression to such an extent that they ate no bread and destroyed each other, eating their victims' hearts instead. Zeus was so appalled at this cannibalism that he sent the Great Flood, or Deluge, to destroy them. Their spirits were banished to the Underworld. As a matter of interest, the year of the Flood in Christian orthodoxy is often set at c2348 BCE. In Greek mythography the date of the Great Flood or Deluge is usually calculated at c1456 BCE.

In the Age of Heroes that followed, Zeus seems to have got it right - just in time for the Trojan Wars and the war against Thebes. These mortals were however very noble and well respected by the gods, some so much so that they became demigods. Most were killed during the wars; however their spirits went to the Elysian Fields, were they received their rewards and lived in peace and happiness.

Finally Zeus created the Iron Age man – the age that persists today. Hesiod did not have anything good to say of this time: *"There will be no favour for the man who keeps his oath or for the just or for the good; but rather men will praise the evil-doer and his violent dealing. Strength will be right and reverence will cease to be; and the wicked will hurt the worthy man, speaking false words against him, and will swear an oath upon them."* It is a gloomy outlook and a time of stress and failing morality. Men deceive each other and lie and no longer feel any shame in doing so. We age quickly and increasingly, evil will triumph and our gods will desert us – until Zeus comes again as the destroyer. Most of this information comes from Hesiod's *"Works and Days"* translated by Hugh G. Evelyn-White.

[Hesiod. The Theogony of Hesiod and Works & Days. Hugh G. Evelyn-White, trs. Create Space Independent Publishing Platform, 2011. Paperback ISBN-13:978-1460936450]

There is another version of the ending of the Bronze Age called the Deucalion myth. Deucalion was one of Prometheus' sons. In this version, Lycaon, King of Pelasgia, sacrificed a child to Zeus, angering the god greatly. Zeus turned the king into a wolf and decided to destroy the impious human race in a great flood. Prometheus warned his son and told him and his wife to build some kind of large chest that could survive the flood. This chest was large enough to hold them and some vital provisions, which enabled them to survive the deluge. After nine days and nights the flood waters started to recede and their boat came to rest on Mount Othrys in Thessaly (or Mount Parnassus in some versions). Deucalion and his wife Pyrrha wept when they saw the desolation and consulted the oracle Themis, asking how they might create a new and hopefully better race of humans. According to Ovid in his *Metamorphoses*, the answer they received was: *"With veiled heads and loosened robes throw behind you as you go the bones of your great mother."*

They were perplexed with the answer. Pyrrha was distraught at the idea of disturbing her mother's bones and wondered why they had been given advice which would certainly displease the gods. After some thought, they both took up stones, representing the "bones" from the earth, (their "great mother,") and cast them behind themselves as they walked. The hard stones started to soften and change shape and take on life: Deucalion's stones became men and Pyrrha's stones became women, thus restoring mankind.

Zeus was not displeased, as he regarded this couple as pious, observant and passionate about mankind. Earth herself regenerated all the other life forms, including the animals, as a result of the restorative rays of the sun meeting the moisture of the drying land. These were the people of the Age of Heroes, if you follow Hesiod's five ages, or, if you follow Ovid, who only records four ages, it was the start of the Age of Iron, the present age. It certainly accounts for man's hard-headedness and determination to survive.

"Is that which is holy loved by the gods because it is holy,
or is it holy because it is loved by the gods?"

Inscribed on the Temple of Apollo in Delphi.

Chapter Five

The Greek Pantheon

There are many other gods that go to make up the full pantheon of Greek mythology and support the intricate structure of the way the Greeks understood their world, but as far as the creation goes, in summary:

· Khaos produced Gaia

· Gaia birthed Uranus, Nyx, Pontus, Erebus and perhaps Aphrodite

· Gaia and Uranus mate and produce many children, the most important being the Titans

· Uranus is unseated by his Titan son, Cronus, who cuts off his father's genitals

· The blood of the genitals falls onto the earth, fertilizing Gaia, who produces more children, among whom are the Giants

· Semen from the genitals falls into the sea, probably creating Aphrodite

· Cronus becomes king, and marries his sister, Rhea

· Cronus is unseated by his son, Zeus, who becomes the god of the Olympians

· Rivalry with the Titans leads to the Titanomachy

· Zeus is victorious and commands the creation of man

· Zeus marries his sister, Hera

· Peace is destroyed by rivalry with the Giants which leads to the Gigantomachy

· Zeus is victorious again and the Olympians rule forever.

The bare bones of it are epic, violent, and driven by power struggles and sexual exploits.

The most important Olympians are: Zeus, Hera, Poseidon, Demeter, Athena, Apollo, Artemis, Ares, Aphrodite, Hephaestus, Hermes, Hestia and Dionysus.

Poseidon's parents were actually Titans and he is often shown with a dolphin, one of his sacred animals, or holding a trident. He is the god of the seas, rivers and horses and is sometimes mistaken for Zeus.

Hera was the Queen of the gods, Zeus' wife and sister. The marriage was tempestuous to say the least. She was extremely jealous and vengeful; this was not surprising, as Zeus was more unfaithful than most husbands. She was the goddess of women, marriage and childbirth. Her sacred animals were the cow and the peacock, and she is often depicted with a crown, a lotus staff or a lion.

Apollo is the only god whose name remains the same in Roman mythology. He was a complex god and very handsome, even beautiful, but always unlucky in love. He was much loved by the gods and was the god of music, prophecy, disease and healing, the sun and education. He is often depicted with a golden lyre or a silver bow and arrows. His most famous romance was when he fell in love with King Priam's daughter, Cassandra. In an effort to win her, he bestowed on her the gift of prophecy. When she finally spurned him, he kissed her goodbye and took away her powers of persuasion. Thereafter, although her prophecies always came true, no one ever believed her.

Artemis, the virgin goddess of the hunt and hunting, was Apollo's twin sister. She was also the goddess of chastity, choirs and the protector of children and wild animals. She is often shown with a bow and arrows, a spear, a lyre or accompanied by a deer. Her particular sacred animals are the deer, bear, wild boar, guinea fowl and quail. She was an intrepid hunter.

Demeter was the goddess of agriculture, grain and bread and the harvest. She taught man how to grow and utilize corn. Her sacred animals are serpents, swine and geckos and she is often shown with a sheaf of corn or a cornucopia. She had several lovers and children but her favorite was her daughter by Zeus, Persephone. Persephone was abducted by Hades and taken in secret to his domain, the Underworld. Demeter was distraught and neglecting all her duties, she searched desperately for her daughter. The crops stopped growing and started to wither and die. and soon the threat of famine hung over the earth. Zeus eventually intervened and struck a deal with Hades that Persephone could return to her mother. As she left, Hades gave Persephone a pomegranate to eat; this induced a spell which compelled her to return to Hades, for three months every year to visit him. This brings our winter, as Demeter once again grieves the loss of her special child.

Hymn to Athena

"I begin to sing of Pallas Athena,
the glorious goddess, bright-eyed, inventive, unbending
of heart,
pure virgin, saviour of cities, courageous, Tritogeneia.
From his awful head wise Zeus himself bare her
arrayed in warlike arms of flashing gold,
and awe seized all the gods as they gazed."

—Homer

Athene or Athena is the goddess of war, heroism, good
council and olives. Her parents were Zeus and his first
wife, Metis. Her birth was extraordinary: an oracle
pronounced that Zeus' first child would be a girl and his
second, a son, who would overthrow him, just as Zeus had
overthrown his own father. When Metis was pregnant
with her first child, Zeus devoured her, hoping to
confound the prophecy. After a while he developed an
intensely painful headache which caused him to scream
out in agony. The other gods gathered about him and
Hermes instructed Hephaestus to split open Zeus' skull
whereupon Athene sprang out, fully clothed and
prodigiously armed. According to Hesiod, Metis had
more brains that all the men put together and this fact,
and the manner in which her daughter was born, destined
Athene to have an abundance of wisdom and intelligence.
She remained a virgin and is usually depicted with a spear,
helmet, and an *aegis,* a round shield decorated with a

picture of Gorgon Medusa and rimmed with images of snakes. Athena was inventive and is credited with producing the first olive tree and several other useful inventions, like a bridle for handling horses. A colossal statue of her, crafted in gold and ivory, stood on the Acropolis in Athens until the 5th century CE when it was removed to Constantinople by the Byzantines -and disappeared somewhere along the way. What a heist that must have been!

Hermes is one of the busiest and most charming of all the gods. The god of travel, trade, thieves, animal husbandry, good luck, and language, he was also a guide to the dead and the herald of the gods. He was a bit of a prankster, but above everything else he was helpful - and there are as many stories of him getting up to mischief as there are of him helping people out of trouble. His father was Zeus and his mother a mountain nymph. He didn't marry, but legend has it that Pan is his son. He once stole Apollo's herd of sacred cattle and reversed their hooves so that the pursuers went in the opposite direction. He invented the lyre, playing dice and the alphabet. He is usually pictured with a winged hat and sandals, carrying a herald's staff.

Ares was a war god, much in the way that Athena was. However, he represented reality of war that required physical aggression and overwhelming force in lieu of Athene's intellectual strategizing. He was the child of Zeus and Hera and was also the god of battle and manliness. His sacred animal was the vulture and sometimes the dog. He was depicted with a helmet, a shield and a spear. He was Aphrodite's lover and in some versions of his story his daughters were the Amazons.

Hestia was the goddess of home, the family, the hearth, meals and sacrificial offerings, as well as architecture. She was the gentlest and mildest of the Olympians, a dedicated virgin and usually shown with a head veil, a branch of the Chaste tree and a kettle. Despite her retiring demeanor, every single meal in a Greek home began and ended with an offering made to her; in many city-states, a hearth in the local temple would be kept always burning for her. She had power of a different kind.

Hephaestus was the only god who was considered ugly and a disabled. In some versions of his creation he was born with a limp, in others he acquired the limp when one of his parents threw him off Olympia Mountain because he was imperfect. His mother was Hera, who is said to have birthed him on her own without Zeus. He became one of the key gods despite all this and was the god of metalwork, blacksmiths, fire, building, sculpture and volcanoes. He fashioned most of the gods' armaments, including the shields belonging to Zeus and Athene. He was very gentle and a patron of the arts. His sacred animals were the donkey and the crane, and he is often depicted as riding a donkey and with an anvil, hammer and tongs to hand. His marriage to Aphrodite was arranged by Zeus; the issue of that union, Ericthonius, was half man and half serpent.

These 12 gods were known as the Olympians and they ruled over all the other gods, the universe and every aspect of human existence. Dionysus, a special case, can be found later.

Achilles speaking to the seer Calchas.

Prophet of evil, when have you ever said
good things to me? You love to foretell the worst,
always the worst! You never show good news.

—Homer; Iliad. Book I

Chapter Six

The Trojan War

The Trojan War is one of the greatest stories of all time. In the 12th and 13th centuries it was regarded as historical fact and consisted of the Greek army, led by Agamemnon, crossing the seas to Sparta in over a thousand ships to demand, or fight for, the return of Menelaus' wife, Helen, who had absconded with Prince Paris. By the mid-19th century it had been relegated to a mythological event. In 1870 an archaeologist named Heinrich Schliemann startled the world by unearthing the ancient city of Troy, the incontestable relics of an ancient, long-running conflict and the remnants of King Priam's treasures at Hisarlik in Turkey. By then, the writings of Eratosthenes, the librarian of the Great Library of Alexandria, had been studied. He had written a Chronography of dates of important events, noting the Trojan War from 1194–1184 BCE. The Schliemann site actually contained many cities built one upon another, and Wilhelm Dörpfeld, who had been Schliemann's young assistant, confirmed level Vll-*a* of the excavations as Homeric Troy in 1893.

If you read the *Iliad* by Homer you will learn a great deal of Greek mythology, especially if you read the back-stories of the heroes involved. The *Iliad* itself only covers 53 days at the end of the 10th year of the war, but the ramifications of the event stretch over 20 years at least.

It all began with a golden apple inscribed with the words: *"For the fairest."* This was a wedding gift, hurled to the floor by Eris, the goddess of Discord, when she discovered that she alone among the gods had not been invited to the wedding of the goddess Thetis, to a worthy mortal, Peleus. Hera, Athene and Aphrodite laid claim to the apple and the Trojan Prince, Paris, was appointed to arbitrate. Athene offered Paris wisdom and the skill of a great warrior if he chose her as the winner; Hera offered him political power and control of the whole of Asia as an inducement; Aphrodite offered him the hand of the most beautiful woman in the world, Helen of Sparta, should he chose her. Paris chose Aphrodite and set off to Sparta, on a "diplomatic mission" to claim his prize, Helen, who just happened to be married to the King of Sparta, Menelaus. As the 20 year epic tale unfolds there are more ramifications than a television soap opera; there are as many betrayals, cliff-hangers, tissue box moments, impossible choices, disastrous decisions and monumental dilemmas as one can imagine, all interspersed with constant interference from the gods (literal moments of "deus ex machina"), to facilitate the developments and outcomes they desire.

Let me illustrate with a few examples.

Aphrodite causes Helen to fall in love with Paris as soon she sets eyes on him. When Menelaus had to attend a state funeral far from home, Paris woos and abducts her and sets off for his home in Troy. There has been much debate over whether Helen went willingly or not and whether she took state assets with her or not.

The seer Calchas made several prophecies about the Trojan war; one of the first being that Troy would only fall if the expedition included the two great warriors Achilles and Odysseus. This caused a delay especially as Odysseus, a shrewd, eloquent and skilled if atypical hero, did not actually want to go. He pretended to be deranged to avoid being conscripted. He was sowing his fields with salt instead of seed as part of faking this madness when the messenger arrived. Unfortunately the conscripting officer placed Odysseus' young son in the path of the plough and when Odysseus took avoiding action, his ruse was revealed. Odysseus reluctantly left his home, knowing it would be twenty years before he returned. Achilles was fifteen years old when he left for the war, with his father's body armor that had been fashioned for him by Hephaestus. He would not return.

A second dreadful pronouncement was that Agamemnon, who led the expedition, had offended the goddess Artemis, and he would have to sacrifice his daughter Iphigenia to her before the becalmed winds would blow allowing the fleet to sail. As the agonized father raised his dagger to deal the fatal stroke a heavy fog descended on the altar. When it cleared Iphigenia's little body had been replaced by a fawn, presumably by Artemis. Hesiod says that Iphigenia became the goddess Hecate.

When the Greeks eventually encamped outside the impenetrable walls of Troy, Paris refused to return Helen and the siege began. This became a way of life for the participants. At one stage, in an effort to break the impasse a duel was arranged between Menelaus and Paris.

"At once, they ceased their attack and fell silent, while Hector spoke to both the armies: 'Listen, you Trojans, and you bronze-greaved Greeks, these are the words of Paris, source of all this strife. He asks that both sides ground their sharp weapons while he and Menelaus, beloved of Ares, fight in single combat between the armies, for Helen and all her treasure. Whichever wins and shows himself the better man let him take both wealth and woman to his house, while the rest of us sign a treaty under oath.'

When he finished, silence reigned, till Menelaus of the loud war-cry spoke: 'Hear me, now. Mine is the heart that suffered most: I propose that Greeks and Trojans part in peace, for you have borne much pain through this quarrel of mine with Paris, though he began it. Whichever of us is fated to die: let him fall; the rest of you shall leave swiftly in peace. Bring two sheep, white ram and black ewe, to sacrifice to Earth and Sun, and we will bring another for Zeus, and let great Priam swear the oath himself ....'

The Greeks and Trojans thrilled to his words, seeing an end to the pain of war. The chariots were reined in along the lines, and the charioteers descended, and shed their battle gear in tightly-spaced piles on the ground. Meanwhile Hector sent two runners to the city to summon Priam and bring the sacrifice. Likewise King Agamemnon sent [one] to the hollow ships, telling him to return with a lamb. He straight obeyed."

—Homer; Iliad. Book III

A great duel took place between the two. Towards the end, when both had lost their weapons, Menelaus "threw himself on Paris, seizing him by his helm's thick horsehair crest, whirled him round and dragged him towards the Achaean lines. Paris was choked by the richly inlaid strap of his helm, drawn tight beneath his chin, pressing on his soft throat. And Menelaus would have hauled him off and won endless glory, had not Zeus' daughter Aphrodite, swift to see it, broken the ox-hide strap, so the empty helm was left in Menelaus' strong grip." [Homer; Iliad. Book III]

The gods even had a hand in the terrible death of the darling of the Trojan War, Achilles. During one of the many attempts on the walls of Troy an arrow from Paris, **guided by Apollo, pierces Achilles' heel**, leading to his death.

Odysseus is the one that finally engineers the end of the war with the deception of the Trojan Horse. Pretending to give up and return home, the Greeks leave "a gift" of a colossal wooden horse for their enemies and retreat out of sight. The horse is drawn into the city and Troy celebrates the end of the siege. In the early hours of the morning, the handpicked warriors hiding inside the horse open the impenetrable gates and Agamemnon finally leads the Greek army into the city and victory. At many points in the story, especially when a god intervenes, the sources record that "it is not yet time" for the event concerned to occur – the timekeeper was perhaps the great Olympian god Zeus, watching with amusement the happenings below.

Electra receives the urn containing her brother's ashes.

"But now, an exile from home and fatherland, thou
hast perished miserably,
far from thy sister; woe is me, these loving hands have
not washed or
decked thy corpse, nor taken up, as was meet, their sad
burden from the flaming pyre.
No! at the hands of strangers, hapless one, thou hast
had those rites,
and so art come to us, a little dust in a narrow urn…

Ah me, ah me! O piteous dust! Alas, thou dear one, sent on
a dire journey,

how hast undone me,- undone me indeed,
O brother mine!"

— Sophocles; Electra.

Chapter Seven

The Influence Of Greek Drama

A major contributing factor affecting how much has come down to us about Greek mythology is the tradition of public discourse, oratory and dramatic presentation in classical Greece. This flourished around the god Dionysus and the many festivals honoring him. Dionysus was the only god who had a mortal mother and said to have been "twice-born." Zeus' lascivious eye fell upon a Theban princess called Semele, and he took to visiting her undercover as a "divine presence" rather than as a man. Once she realized she was pregnant by him, she made Zeus promise to grant her one wish, which he did. She asked to see him as he was in his immortal form and she died in a great burst of flaming glory as he revealed himself in all his power and majesty. Zeus retrieved the fetal child and stitched him into his thigh to carry him to term. Zeus' wife, Hera, in a fit of jealous rage, dispatched a few Titans to rip the child to pieces. However the goddess Rhea brought him back to life and presented him to Zeus. Zeus became particularly enchanted with this child and sent him to be raised in safety by the nymphs of Mount Nysa. *Dios* means "of Zeus" and so he was named Dionysus.

Dionysus is credited with inventing the art of viticulture. He was the god of fertility, wine, ritual madness, pleasure, festivity, parties and the theatre. His sacred animals are the leopard, lynx and tiger and very specifically, the sexually potent goat; especially the satyrs, who were half man and half goat. He travelled widely and was generally regarded as the "bad boy" of Olympus. Once he was abducted by pirates who didn't realize his powers. He changed the ship's mast into a massive vine and the sails dripped with wine. He turned himself into a lion and with the help of a bear, *"he dispatched the pirate captain. In terror, the remaining crew members leapt overboard and were changed into dolphins."* He spared the helmsman, as he had been the only one who had voted against Dionysus being "press-ganged," and they sailed on to Naxos.

Several festivals were held in his honor, all of which typically involved a great deal of eating, drinking and dancing in enormous street parties. Devotees dressed in goat skins pretended to be satyrs and behaved like them. There were parades of worshipers carrying phallic objects through the streets of Grecian city-states; the more devout would literally become deliriously drunk and indulge in sexual orgies and other debaucheries. The most important event by far though was held in Athens, from the 9th to the 13th of March, every year. It was called the City Dionysia, and took the form of a great literary competition for writers, particularly dramatists. The greatest writers of the day took part.

Aeschylus lived from 525–456 BCE and wrote tragedies that won many prizes at the Dionysia. We have 7 surviving texts: *Agamemnon; The Choephori; Eumenides; The Persians; Prometheus Bound; The Seven Against Thebes* and *The Suppliants*. He was also an actor and there was an attempt to assassinate him on stage as a result of initiation rituals he had revealed: the Eleusinian Mysteries, used in the cult of Demeter and Persephone. "*Agamemnon*" won first prize in 458 BCE and tells the story of his return to his wife Clytemnestra after the Trojan Wars. Clytemnestra kills him and Cassandra, the mistress he brings back with him, with her own hands, in revenge for his sacrifice of Iphigenia.

Sophocles (496–409 BCE) was also an actor, and he is remembered as the tragedian who extended the number of actors used in a play and was thus able to take the themes beyond a dialogue about religion and morality into an interactive dramatic performance. He wrote well over 100 plays of which seven complete texts survive: *Antigone; Electra; Oedipus at Colonus; Oedipus the King, Philoctetes and Trachinian Women*. He was 28 when he won first place at the Dionysia, dislodging Aeschylus. "*Electra*" was written quite late in his life and must be one of the most moving of the tragedies. Electra was Agamemnon's daughter and Iphigenia's sister. She had sent her beloved brother into hiding soon after Agamemnon departed for the Trojan Wars, when she suspected he might be in danger from her mother's lover, Aegisthus. The play "*Electra*" deals with the revenge she takes on her mother and Aegisthus when they kill Agamemnon on his return from Troy. The extract above occurs when she is told her brother has been killed and she receives his ashes and realizes that she alone must exact the revenge.

Euripedes was born in 480 BCE and was also a prolific poet and dramatist. He wrote about 90 plays, of which 17 survive. He first entered the City Dionysia in 455 BCE and won a first prize in 441 BCE, the first of four. He also based much of his work on popular myths of the time but he was more critical of the content than others, and he was known for developing complex female protagonists like Medea, Hecuba and Andromache. He also wrote a play on the Electra story. His most powerful texts were *Medea, Hippolytus, Alcestis and The Bacchae*. He died in Macedonia in 406 BCE. *"The Bacchae"* is about Dionysus, who returns to the city of his birth, Thebes, to vindicate his mother Semele and to claim acknowledgement as one of the gods. Essentially, it is a serious play about reason versus irrationality. It won a fifth first prize at the City Dionysia for Euripides posthumously.

One of the requirements governing the Dionysia was that any writer who entered had to present at least one satirical play or a substantial comedy.

Aristophanes (c456–c380 BCE) is the best remembered gifted writer of comedies. He wrote 30 plays but only eleven texts have survived. He is best remembered for *"The Birds,"* in which he satirized the idea of democracy; *"The Clouds"*; a serious critical attack on Sophocles, and *"Lysistrata"* in which he mocked war. The latter is still often performed today and still carries a bite; in a bid to end the Peloponnesian Wars, Lysistrata convinces all the women to withhold sex from their men until a peace treaty is negotiated. The women also take over the treasury on the Akropolis in order to control the finances that facilitate the war.

Chapter Eight

Two Greek Mortal Heroes In Mythological Tales

Theseus and the Slaying of the Minotaur. In the *Iliad*, Nestor says that among all the heroes of the Trojan War, none was greater than Theseus. Theseus was a mortal famous for many deeds of valor, including killing the Centaur of Minos on Crete. The creature was half man and half bull and was born to Queen Pasiphae after Zeus had visited her in the form of a bull. There are many variations in this particular myth and in some versions the bull was actually a gift to Minos from the god Poseidon. King Minos of Crete felt he couldn't kill the creature, so he imprisoned him in an elaborate labyrinth he had designed by the famous architect Daedalus. This maze provided a convenient way of disposing of his enemies as well as feeding the centaur that only ate human flesh. Unfortunately when Minos' son Androgeus went to the games in Athens, he was killed by the same bull that had visited his mother. In his anger and grief, King Minos demanded an annual tribute from Athens in the form of 7 young men and 7 young women to be sacrificed to the Minotaur. The King of Athens, in fear of the dreaded might of Minos, complied for the first two years. In the third year his son Theseus commits himself to end this dreadful situation and, very much against his father King Aegeus' wishes, he volunteers himself as a sacrifice and sets sail. The King makes him promise that if he survives, he will set white sails on his return home. Theseus announces his intention of killing the Minotaur to King Minos and his daughter, Ariadne, realizes that even if Theseus succeeds in killing the dreaded beast, he will still perish trying to find his way out of the labyrinth. She gives him a ball of wool to unwind as he seeks the monster's den and to follow on the way back. She also asks him to take her with him when he goes home. Theseus is able to overcome the monster and find his way back to the entrance and he sets sail for home, taking Ariadne with him. They have a difficult voyage home, fighting really bad weather and tempestuous storms, requiring many of the sails to be repaired and replaced, using the spare set of black sails. King Aegeus, keeping watch from a high cliff outlook, sees the black sails on the horizon and, thinking his son is lost, casts himself into the raging sea below. Ever since that day that sea is called the Aegean in honor of his grief.

Jason and the Golden Fleece. Jason came to fame as a hero before the Trojan War. Pelias usurped the throne of Iolcus (present day Volos) by imprisoning his brother, Aeson, the rightful heir. He received a warning from an oracle that a descendent of Aeson would take revenge on him and he sends Jason, Aeson's son, on a quest to retrieve the Golden Fleece. The Golden Fleece was the skin of a ram sacred to Zeus that was kept in the Temple of Ares, the god of war, and guarded by an impressive dragon, in the land of Colchis. Aeson presumed that Jason would meet his death on the journey as this was regarded as an impossible mission. Jason was bright as well as intrepid and he gathered around him a band of 50 warriors including, in some versions of the story, great heroes like Heracles. A fine ship was built and named Argo after the designer, Argus, and after suitable blessings were sought the men set forth. This mission became known as the Argonautica. After an adventurous journey, charting the waters of the Black Sea for the first time, they arrived in Colchis and requested the prize from the ruler King Aeetes, in the name of the goddess Hera. Not wanting to give up the prize but hesitant to displease the gods, King Aeetes sets Jason a prohibitive trial: yoke two fire-breathing bulls with metallic legs, plough a large field and then sow the field with dragon's teeth. He neglected to tell him that this would result in an army of warriors rising from the earth that would tackle him and his paltry party. Fortunately, the King's daughter, Medea, was impressed with Jason and, being a bit of a sorceress and the granddaughter of the sun god Helios, (and really very bad news if only he had known!) she gave him a protective potion to make him impermeable to fire and iron for 24 hours. She also told him about her father's plan and what to do about it. When the army rose from the ground Jason threw a large stone into their midst; thinking it was an attack, the men turned on each other and they fought to the death, eliminating each other completely. Aeetes had to give Jason permission to retrieve the Golden Fleece, hoping this time that the dragon would slay him. Medea stepped in again and put a spell on the dragon so that Jason was able to retrieve the sacred prize with ease. As

Jason and the Argonauts boarded the Argo and prepared to depart, Medea abducted her brother and then joined them. As they sailed away, she killed her brother and cut him to pieces, spreading his body parts in the way of the perusing ship. This slowed Aeetes, as he tried to retrieve all the bits and pieces of his son. Many years later, in another great myth, Medea would kill her own children that she had with Jason. But this story belongs to the brave Jason and his Argonauts. After many further trials and tribulations he lays the precious Golden Fleece at the feet of King Pelias.

Conclusion

Greek mythology is complex, and although the creation of mortals seems to have been an afterthought and embarked upon mainly for the vast entertainment of the Olympians, as these myths developed, an intense interaction between gods, demi-gods and heroic and no- so heroic mortals manifests. The heritage of the great Classical Period from c480 to 323 BCE, which includes the famous philosophers and the great dramatic playwrights, is certainly germane to us all to this very day. By 336 BCE Greek language, literature, culture and religious beliefs were appreciated throughout the civilized world and certainly anywhere touched by Alexander the Great. In 192 BCE the Spartan monarchy collapsed and Sparta came under Roman rule; by 168 BCE, Perseus, the last king of Macedonia, also fell under the Roman yoke.

It is a mistake to think that the Romans simply took over Greek mythology, though most of the Greek gods do have a Roman counterpart. The Roman gods had a very different kind of persona and the syncretization of the two beliefs involved a complex and sometimes conflicted process. Still, in 145 BCE Greece became part of the Roman Empire. I wonder what Zeus had to say about that?

"Myths are public dreams, dreams are private myths."

—Joseph Campbell; American mythologist 1904-1987

87913621R00029

Made in the USA
San Bernardino, CA
08 September 2018